Bleat & Prattle

Bleat & Prattle

poems

D. Walsh Gilbert

Clare Songbirds
Publishing House

Clare Songbirds Publishing House Poetry Series
ISBN 978-1-957221-22-9
Clare Songbirds Publishing House
Bleat & Prattle © 2025 D. Walsh Gilbert

Printed in the United States of America
FIRST EDITION

cover image *Winters Breath,* courtesy of Joshua Fuller (2017)
from Unsplash.

140 Cottage Street
Auburn, New York 13021
www.claresongbirdspub.com

Dedicated to my daughters,
Emily and Meredith

Contents

When I was small and stayed quiet
some animals came
new ones each time
and waited there near me
and all night they were eating the black

— W.S. Merwin, "Animals from Mountains"

Visiting my Thin Place

I'm familiar with liminal space and that slender invisible
slippage between here and there where a body can
disappear like a rabbit into underbrush, the one

who gets away. Now, I focus on graceful liminal time,
that shift of energy between summer and autumn
nearly imperceptible while in a melancholic trance

of vivid details—the bronzing of a leaf, the whir
of the last hummingbird, the frantic lust of yellow jackets
on ruptured apples, the gloaming dawn & auroral sunset

as disorienting as the early darkening or some scurf
of nest-building too late in the chill. To get my bearings
I visit the meadow with pen and binoculars to harvest

fodder from the pastureland with its burrowing mole.
I, too, consume the liminal blind, skitter among rough edges,
feast on grub & earthworm, then dig deeper underground.

There in the minutiae is a single grain of crystal quartz
faceted like salt and just as transparent—a solid hexagonal
able to imbed inside my small finger, and without hesitation

I let it. How quick is the slippage. This conchoidal scrap
—like a scallop shell— this shred of white sand riverbed
brings me back to the beginning. To a fragile flint beginning.

Realizing I am Rabbit Fur

The hollow-mold rabbit lamp with bone-
porcelain skin thin as fingernail
stares motionless through my window
pane. A life-sized night
light, she waits patiently
and casts a shadow on the windowsill.
The sun always goes down.
She glows with a simple switch.

*

Once the Velveteen Rabbit had become,
all ear twitch and hop and able
to visit cabbage and radish, she turned
toward moss, so abundant
in the forest, and to prickly ferns
which uncurl slowly. The mosses
named her, and together they laid
in blue-green shadow, side-by side.

*

With Alice, I follow the ghost-white
rabbit, its waistcoat and pocket watch,
but when I drop my spectacles,
I see that rabbit in the month's full moon,
its dark shadow in the light,
tattered edges soft as loom-
woven layers split down the middle—
that's how velvet's made.

Resolution

I've built myself a room
        of soft-pulp paper walls.
One side ruffles in a relentless north wind.

Two walls are crumple-wrinkled with cuticle-chewed
corners—paper flattened once again after discard.

The fourth wall is missing—rather, opens into space
and leads deeper into my house:
                to a kitchen, a hallway,
to a paneled Dutch door sealed
into a single-solid piece and bolt-locked safe.

An artist would draw on these paper walls.
Could a poet
write an epic? I wonder if the stories
        belong to me in the end.

There's a meadow out there
        beyond the paper, beyond the weeping
willow and the fountain grass.
        There, I planted golden daffodils.

There, bees come, and wasps,
straight from their hex-chambered, paper nests
        made from gnawed
wood fiber and their own saliva.

I long to be a wasp, to communicate with stinger.

Tonight, dazzled by rogue sunsets
                        and rebellious silence,
I'll begin to scribble myths. Tell me it's easy
to erase an errant smudge
penciled onto paper walls,
        to erase until it tears through.

Tell me I could walk through that torn hole to where
the bees teach their story-dance
        and map the way to nectar.

Right now, my walls are blank. But every night,
when I click the lights off, one at a time,
and the darkness darkens,
          my silhouette
                    —that shadow on the paper walls
which anyone could see from the street—
will disappear.

The words will remain
written with the blackened wick of candlelight
          or etched by my stinger.

The Time of Balance

The dawn air has a northern lash to it,
an elephant gray trample, and heavy

with garden soil eddied upward, swirling,
the crone soup of autumn equinox

thinning the earth-veil, and it's the way—
The scarlet cardinal tips in flight, tries

to catch the holly bough sway... and then,
it's the holding on. Quartz-white lightning

flashes his feathers, reddens his red
into a dragon fire which fights back,

thundering—the stiff refusal of a small thing
who tastes winter's vaulted wind on his beak

and still opens his mouth. He swallows
the tempest. And when the azure west-blue

sky breaks on the horizon, he welcomes it
with muffled feather shake and happy chatter

as if nothing beyond ordinary's happened.

After *Morning, Going to Work*
—Vincent van Gogh, (Netherlands) 1890

These stable legs don't slip.
Whether ridden, walking,

or carried—as wobbly
full as Mother Mary had been—

knock-kneed, aching legs
of burden plod to work.

No one notices the poppies.
No one notices the rhythm

steps make as if a lullaby
or in a cradle. Here, no one

yanks the halter. There's
just going, rope slack,

legs buckling a little,
sickle tucked, basket empty.

Conscripted to move forward
by hunger while clutching

the mane of a beast able
to survive on chicory & thatch.

Honest donkey, wife,
and blue-clothed man,

foot-shod, hauling a pitch-
fork and its inky tines.

His craggy legs are set
in the same aspect

as the donkey's—
crooked as a poet's thumb.

The Ars Poetica of the Friesian

He takes the bit between his teeth,
tastes the foreign language
learned before his birth.
His lips part willingly,
and he chews the connection,
swallows the obedience of it,
rolls its messages along his tongue.

Through the leather reins,
his taut enjambed line,
his ear tips to listen
to the twitch of his rider's finger.
He forgives
the snaffle which bends
and flexes like the link
of a locomotive to its train.
He's the locomotive.
He could power through but chooses
to accept its pinch.
He spits the irritation of it.

And when a hen flaps her wings
at a thieving magpie,
his rider's thigh presses
and pledges their body united.
He circles past,
and trots the long side
like a molten nocturne.

Ophelia, from the water

Damn this cloud of patriarchal breath. It holds me.
I long to excavate a resting place—
to dredge down and deep into my eternity.
Here, surface-wrought, with ripples warping
birdsong and splashes blurring vision,
I'm sheltered from my own, authentic cold. Velvet
cloak, petticoat of linen, silk bodice
spun from the spit of mulberry moths—
all these betray my penetrating voyage.
The weavings lift me—and obedient—I float.
Stalled minutes fight against subtraction,
refuse my absence. Skirts spread.
My hair hovers atop these amniotic waters
as if a caul of fragility—its many
threads.
         You there, happy frog, not a hair
on you, lithe and slippery, naked & able
to spring on cock-bent legs from stone
to riverbank, sodden and yet not, you understand
the visions of the bottom sludge
which coats a body with its silted warmth. Tell
the mud to polish my unwelcomed skin,
to hone spine and throat razor sharp,
but leave unfilled my mouth, with its prior-to
un-listened femininity. When I finally utter
the lie, *I'm not afraid*, you'll hear
the scream that long-lived silence makes.

Voyages

I'm the child of a survivor of New York City's
soot-blackened subway. My mother, an able rat,
could navigate the welded sidewalk grates
while chipping coins into a busker's cup. She could
scamper on the granite concourse curb,
dodge pigeon shit and feathers—and never fall.
The gutter wouldn't frighten her. She gnawed.

I've always wanted to fill my trouser pockets
with visions of living—of cloud and leathered mountain.
But when the gusts of winter threaten and swell,
I flee like an elk driven from its peak and rocky
elevation by a wicked north wind—leaving
what's been familiar. Will I find a fallow cornfield?
Though grateful for the stalk and scatter, would
my pockets, pulled inside-out, soon empty?

I'll hitch down New Hampshire's gravel road
to Gloucester's fishing port. Fat lines, strung from
grappling hook and trawler, promise to speak to me
what's spoken undersea. A nomadic gray whale,
itinerate, hungry, sifting the microscopic
from the gull-brine of these waters, blows
salt into my hair. It curls. Every wispy strand
heads in its own direction.

Perhaps, I should settle in the entanglement
made of twig, moss, and bird spit. I could teeter
on branches shrouded in leaf, hoping to be unseen.
Windswept in a rooted home. There—safety—
ducking in and out of shadow. I could be
held in the curved hand of a warbler's cup,
socketed and secure, the gales of ancestral migration
a final sigh.

How do I recognize the perfect destination—
the final acre of land able to anchor the wandering
of discontented feet? These hills are made of malleable clay.
My name, engraved on a granite monument, undated,
is waiting in the rain. In the graveyard, there are fences
cast from iron. And I'm wary of the thorn
on brambles—with neither sunken root nor climbing
blossom. Simply braided rope meant to bind me.

Approaching Seventy

"You become. It takes a long time."
—Margery Williams, *The Velveteen Rabbit*

I am remembering
the small things
now that I am
the old woman at the shore,
someone
connected by her roots,
an oyster
clinging to a rock
swallowing sea-
water's brine
and spitting out
slow stories,
little words.
The weeds of the abyss,
ripped out,
hang from my neck,
hag hair
riotously
scattered
like ancestral rays:
sunlight
moonlight
starlight,
those small things
which pierce and sting
and make.
I can see
the falling acorn
crack its shell
and bury.
I can see
how I fit in
the selkie's
ragged skin.

Lughnasadh

Cow parsley circles the foot
of a sea-blue spruce like so many
flower-girls surrounding a bride.
Not even the rain can dampen them.

The month for shaking clean
the burlap bags is past: the July of empty
yesterdays. Upon us: new spuds
plentiful in every trench and hill.

We practice tapping a half-hardy
pumpkin, listening for hollow,
pinching for rot. Heft the rugged
from the field. A soup is simmering.

The many vagaries of light: the sun
and shade and candlelight—fire
in a hearth, and hearts becoming jackdaw,
rook, the growl of wagon crawl.

The drumlin mushrooms thrive
under compost, white as they bulge,
white as August's wild carrot,
pure as pignut, dropwort, angelica,

while the sea-fog breathes out loud
and Slieve Gullion speaks
the evergreen lilts of legend, and myth,
and crow song in the edgelands.

Samhain

The farming men are cutting the dead
hedges for the Samhain bonfire—
the bone-fire. For the culling of the old
and the coming of the new, they winnow

the worn and the sick from the herd,
the unwanted bones moaning toward fire—
the stags and empty freemartins,
the non-milkers and the lame.

But six taut udders in Armagh escape,
and we can't speak of the Sídhe
but the Púca is about,
and the old hag on Inishbofin laughs

as four black Aberdeen Angus cows
and two lusty Red Ruby heifers
are swallowed by the thin land
beside the Derrynoose chapel. They low,

We are beastly wombs, unleashed.

And with wide hips of great swaying arches,
driven by the scent of under,
they go where the world as they know it
loses color, but softens,

to where the graves are open and time
stands still, and cattle can slip
like a full moon toward November,
like bonfire smoke between raindrops.

Imbolc: 'in the belly'

The lambs are dropping onto field and hill,
warm-wet steaming, ewes astonished.

The rocks on Slieve Gullion are happy.
They don't mind the uninvited mess.

There's no barbed wire here,
and soon more sheep will be walking where

yesterday was mirror-glassy ice.
I've come to watch all these goddesses

soon to be crowned with primrose and dandelion.
It makes me anxious when the lambs

try to stand, to wobble-find the teat,
then finally wag their tails, so sure

this is where they belong—on sedge or bracken,
unafraid of slipping through the fissures

in basalt, or the scratch of blackthorn, or the misty
foggy-cloud which some consider soft.

Belly quivering, one ewe stands for the birth.
The baby plummets, dazed into living.

I've come across an ocean to see this.

The Little Hills of Monaghan
for my family there

When I see a mother
cup her newborn's head
and rub
her palm across his crown,
instinctively,
I breathe in—
a scent remembered,
the musky wax of birth,
a tinge
of spilled milk.

*

This, the same scurf smell
scuffed from the drumlins
of Kavanagh's
Inniskeen Road
as he walked.
Pollen dust
and last night's mist
clinging to the hedges
and thickening
the bog-rich earth.

*

The Irish Times confirms
gold was found in drill holes
in Clontibret,
lodes and ore assured,
mining to begin.
And the scalp
of the Cailleach's child
will peel back.
And Kavanagh is rising
from his grave, keening
a lament
the threatened corn crake understands.

A Honeybee in Connecticut

Whether nectar-drunk, lost, or simply disoriented,
a honeybee, buzzing louder than its small body
should be able to, bumps my window's glass
                            again and again.
It can't free itself from behind the double-
glazed wall despite an opening only inches
to its left. It can see the field, the leafy
hydrangea vine climbing the wall, sees the way
it came; yet something invisible holds it back.

I free it from its misery, cranking the casement
wider, the opening now more & more impossible
to miss, until the bee catches the summer freshness,
escapes on the eddy of a breeze.
                        I could have shut
the window just as easily. Trapping it between
the pane and window screen, I could have
closed this honeybee closer to my world, listened
to its stumble, heard its confusion in wing beats.

I could have kept it to myself. But,
it deserved to find its own hive, to churn
royal jelly and feed it to its queen. I understand
that vital urgency, that need to be complete:
it's why my daughters settled in the West. And look,
a dust of pollen on the sill.

To a Spider in its Web

You have claimed this foggy corner
of my home
as your own
world, your whole
world, tethering sash
to door frame.
You've chosen
the crack
where kitchen warmth
leaks out in winter,
and calls
to nest-seeking beetles
and frost-weary flies—
any living bit to stick
to your threads
until surrender gasps.
Tendrils entangle us
the harder we struggle.
You, on the solid board
at the sidelight window,
you stretch
to where my hand has only touched.
A fragile reaching.
Little orb-weaver
with your lines
of spinneret silk,
your home
of filament
is so different from mine—
so delicate,
so intricate,
so ephemeral.
Each strand's a glimpse
of possibility,
and I don't know
how to open
my door now
without destroying it.

Age 84 in Dog-Years

In the month of Queen Anne's Lace,
he sits on his haunches
behind the fence—
my old dog,
the animal equivalent of a crumbling
barn, its stalls left open,
the horses gone.

Stone deaf and half blind,
he sniffs what's familiar.
Remember when making your way
to the shore as a kid?
the scent of sun-warm marsh
and salt? of August?
of summer nearly over?

A dog and Queen Anne's Lace,
two strangers who know
each other very well.
He wants
to hobble into the tall grass,
but I don't want
to open the gate.

Outbound

The dog is staring at the kitchen wall again.
I don't know where he's gone.
     I'm waiting.

Any minute, his splayed feet will slip beneath him.
His eyes will face the red-clay tile and wooden baseboard.
     The wall

and floor meet at a perfect corner,
and he can't get enough of this map-emptied air.
     Tomorrow will be

his forever sleep. Some say a final upward
rush. Only then can his head and deadened legs
     re-quicken,

now entranced by the wall as if
encountering a door with a knocker too high
     to reach.

Last night, I dreamed about a Green Line streetcar.
I landed at the station just as it arrived.
     No waiting.

All the passengers were Labrador retrievers,
and I knew the names of each of them.
     I stepped

on-board, into *a small unfocused blur, a standing chill.*

Losing Footing

Heartbreaking, how that wild turkey hobbles,
his leg crippled in some accident, unwitnessed,
life-changing, instantaneous, incidental.

His skeleton, built from Talcott Mountain
clay, has a break in its mortar. The place
meant to hold things together bends off-center.

Who knows if the turkey remembers how he walked
before. Who knows if he knows what's coming,
what possibilities exist around the fence's corner.

He shakes winter from his feathers, pecks
between the glaucous bluestone pavers for what's
unseen. My touch would be gentle, and yet

intolerable. As winds churn sumac and forsythia,
he's on his path. I'm on mine. Comfort, though,
if I could hold his gargoyle face holy-ugly

as any sinner. I would kiss the cheek of what's
a god—forgiven for my rude trespass—rub
against what is elusive, absorb the covenant

dark solstice promises, hear the hunting sniff
of the coyote questioning a hollow log,
                                    and still shuffle on,
flight feathers a clay-mud umber of burnished radiance.

In Response to "Beautiful Short Loser"
—Ocean Vuong, *Time is a Mother*

Ocean, my tree is a grand-*mother*,
an apple tree at least a hundred
years old, supporting birdhouse,
feeder, prayer to Brigid who
also weathers rain. My body

has always been too big, lush
as its green land of origin.
Green voices in the rain, green rain in the voices,
so you said. The last poem in

my collection says *I am a cage,*
in search of a bird. A finch to light
in this apple tree I keep—I keep
tending—grandmother reappearing
plump and rosy-red each September.

Cats Can Meow the Same Frequency as Babies: an erasure

They'd been living in the hollow of a rotted cottonwood.
Within minutes, two feral kittens, born to tuxedo
cats and abandoned, catch the scent
of salmon left inside the Have-a-Heart which snaps up
their fragile cries and matted fur, tight and secure.
They hadn't had a drop of milk in days.

Hollow.

Within   feral kittens
      abandoned,
                      a heart   snaps
                     in days.

Housebound after her hysterectomy,
with double-hung windows opened wide,
my daughter hears the two of them bawl. Every body
enfolds the essence of an animal.

               Catch the scent.
      Left inside,
—fragile—
              a drop of milk.

The Turn of September: a reverse erasure

I am
                downwind,
not even
        a sip from
                    the apple
    sweet.
                            The shade
                        clinging   a bit—
        my human-ness
    (lemon,
                            a-blur)
                    acting so.

                *

I am quiet—I sit here melancholy-rigid
on this bench, downwind, hidden,

not even blinking, as a migrating hum-
mingbird takes a sip from the feeder.

It flits from a perch on the apple branch,
passing me, passing the birdbath,

the sweet hibiscus, the shade
of the dogwood still clinging a bit

to its pink. Surely, the bird can smell me,
my human-ness not covered

by lemon morning body spray. But wait—
it buries into a petunia, wings a-blur

a 2-inch whir of feather and beak
vibrating skin-silk petals, acting so alive.

And the dogwood berries feed the dark-
eyed juncos I now notice forage overhead,

quivering as I do, but wildly filled.

the rest of my days I spend
wandering: wondering
what, anyway,
was that sticky infusion, that rank flavor of blood,
that poetry, by which I lived?

—Galway Kinnell, "The Bear"

Notes

"After *Morning, Going to Work*"
The painting which inspired this poem is by Vincent van Gogh, (Netherlands) 1890:

https://commons.wikimedia.org/wiki/File:Vincent_van_Gogh_-_Morning,_going_out_to_Work.jpg

"Lughnasadh"
Lughnasadh, pronounced LOO-nah-sah, is a festival in Ireland marking the beginning of the harvest season. It's celebrated on August 1 and is still widely observed.

"Samhain"
The origin of Halloween, Samhain, pronounced SAH-win, marks the end of the harvest season in Ireland and the beginning of the darker half of the year. It's celebrated on November 1.

"Imbolc: 'in the belly' "
Imbolc, pronounced IM-bolk, is also known as Saint Brigid's Day in Ireland. It marks the beginning of spring and is celebrated on the first of February.

"The Little Hills of Monaghan"
Newspaper reports about the discovery of gold deposits in Clontibret in County Monaghan, Ireland can be found in *The Irish Times:* https://www.irishtimes.com/business/2022/10/06/conroy-gold-confirms-gold-mineralisation-deposits-at-clontibret-operation/

"Outbound"
The last line of this poem is from the poem, "Aubade", by Philip Larkin: https://www.poetryfoundation.org/poems/48422/aubade-56d229a6e2f07

Acknowledgements

The Field Guide Magazine	"Age 84 in Dog Years"
	"A Honeybee in Connecticut"
	"In Response to 'Beautiful Short Loser'"
Hole in the Head Review	"Lughnasadh"
	"Samhain"
	"Approaching Seventy"
The Inflectionist Review	"Visiting My Thin Place"
KAIROS	"The Little Hills of Monaghan"
New Feathers Anthology	"Cats Can Meow the Same Frequency as Babies: an erasure"
Rockvale Review	"To a Spider in its Web"
Stone Poetry Quarterly	"The Ars Poetica of the Friesian"
	"The Time of Balance"
	"Voyages"

For their sustaining aid and support, encouragement, and honest critique while writing this poetry, I am forever grateful to the members of the Partners in Poetry workshop, the Farmington Valley Chapter of the Connecticut Poetry Society, and as always, family and friends who have read the poems in early drafts with love and guidance, especially my husband who first read this collection and believed in it and believes in me.

I could never simply thank my reviewer, Steve Straight, retired professor of English and former director of the poetry program at Manchester Community College in Connecticut. His thoughts on the entirety of this chapbook overwhelm me. His generosity is truly appreciated.

And gratitude is not enough to extend to *The Field Guide Magazine*, and its editor, Amanda Marrero, who nominated the poem, "In Response to 'Beautiful Short Loser' ", for a Pushcart Prize in poetry. The journal itself is truly a work of art, and I am so honored to be included.

~DWG

About the Author

D. Walsh Gilbert is a dual citizen of the United States of America and Ireland. Her poetry collections include *Ransom, imagine the small bones,* and *Finches in Kilmainham,* and *Misneach* (all, Grayson Books), *Once the Earth had Two Moons* (Cerasus Poetry), *[M]AR[Y]* (Kelsay Books), and *Deirdre* (Impspired). Her poems appear widely in poetry journals online and in print. She serves on the board of the Riverwood Poetry Series and as co-editor of the *Connecticut River Review* published by the Connecticut Poetry Society with which she manages the Farmington Valley workshop program.

Gilbert lives in Farmington, Connecticut on a former sheep farm at the foot of the Talcott Mountain near the watershed of the Farmington River, previously the homelands of the Tunxis and Sukiaugk peoples and near the oldest site of human occupation in Connecticut, dating back 12,500 years. She welcomes turkey, deer, bear, and bobcat as daily visitors from the forest behind her home, writes every day, and visits her family in County Monaghan, Ireland as often as possible.